REVERBERANCE

RAMESH CHANDRA PRADHANI

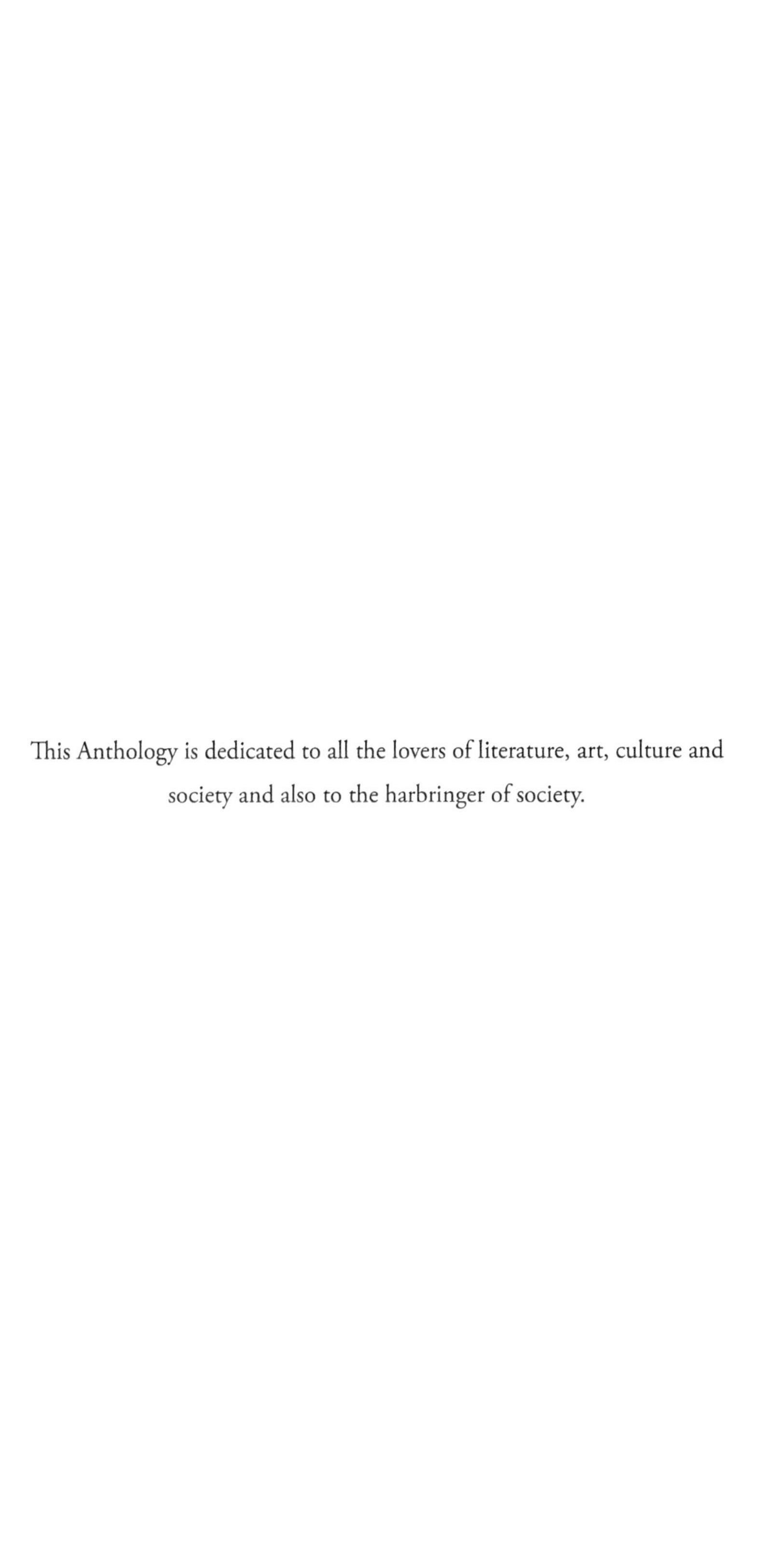

This Anthology is dedicated to all the lovers of literature, art, culture and society and also to the harbringer of society.

Contents

Contents

Contents

Contents

Contents

Foreword

In the long traverse of life from the start to end of life we experience moments and actions both better and bitter. And a man either swayed by the adversities or overpowered by pomp and and luxury forgetting the ethos of life staggers on the path and for him the destination remains a distant dream. On the other hand one equipped with valour and determination, perseverance and resilience is a hero in the battle of life. What does afford essence to take life to the climax of success and glory ? I would say firmly that it is nothing but the persons all around are the springs of inspiration to show the noble path. Sometimes their worthy words through their creativity work wonders to bring a transition in life. Now I shall cite the Anthology of Poems 'REVERBERANCE' by my dear friend Ramesh Chandra Pradhani as a laudable creation to delight the heart, soar the spirit and shield the confidence of the readers. The effort of blending myriads of thoughts together to energise the hearts needs to be praised with immense applause. I cannot but appreciate his enthusiasm and hard work that have given him an uncommon place and high honour. I am sure the variegated themes of the poems originating from his endless store of emotion might touch millions of hearts for transformation.

Durbadal Ghibela
Reader in Englidsh
Jarasingha College,Jarasingha
Dist -Balangir (Odisha)

Preface

Life is full of reverberance sometimes sweet, sometimes bitter. Moreover, life is an amalgam of sorrows and joys, negativity and positivity, success and failure, rise and fall and so on. Without the presence of one, the other is incomplete to flourish and can not be conducive to the society where one lives and things around him. Naturally the dark side of life very often closes the door of entering into the arena of reality but sometimes it makes life purposeful and meaningful. The compromise of the religion and science, conciliation between inferiority and superiority creates a bridge of hope and faith.

The present Anthology of poems REVERBERANCE is a solution to all the social economic, religious, cultural, educational, political issues confronting the whole mankind. Amidst the painful and terrific happenstances, life is to survive when each poem in this Anthology stands as a safeguard to the peaceful and prosperous level and helps sustaining love, harmony, sympathy and solidarity.

Ramesh Chandra Pradhani

Acknowledgements

Most of the poems of this anthology are highly appreciated by the poets, critics and awarded with prizes, certificates and medals. Some poems are already published in verious nationally and internationally distinguished facebook poetry forums. The present anthology is nothing but the collection of already published poems.

In bringing out the book form the whole hearted support and inspiration of my family members are highly solicited. The helping hands of Mr. Durbadal Ghibela, Reader in English, Jarasingha College, Jarasingha and Bimal Kathar can never be ignored.

Ramesh Chandra Pradhani

Prologue

The Reverberance, An Anthology of poems-Volume-VI
The breath and finer spirit of my heartfelt expression
Replete with love, peace, joy, hope, faith and gratification
Enriched with courage, knowledge and rejuvenation
Gives the slogans of unity, integrity, justice and equality
For the establishment of humans morality and humanity.
Ramesh Chandra Pradhani

1. POWER OF SMILE

Lily of euphoria blooms
In the pond of heart when mindset of moon appears in the starry sky
Open heart smile melts away the snow of frozen mind
Flowers of emotions abundantly ripples heart inside
Often subdues the naughtiness of indifferent soul
Can haul the mountains of silence to console
Rainbow of ecstasy seen in the azure of gap
Bridging the two sides of East and West to reshape
A new and noble world of bliss emerges in the wasteland
Everything happens miraculously before you comprehend.

2. TOGETHER WE STAND

Under the canopy of the vastness of clean sky

On the middle of the road of life we stand to fly

Amidst the serene loneliness spreading around the horizon

The path is moving ahead towards the destination.

We are in the centre in the beautiful creation of the Almighty

For a purpose we are left here with a resolute ambition

No matter nobody or nothing is with us for accompany

But we are blessed with His grace and power in adversity to stand for justice and harmony.

Let's breathe deep to embrace the silhouette of the pristine wind

Listen to the symphony of nature's generosity

Calmness of the time crooning the poetry of His sanctity

How lucky we are here to enjoy the effulgent beauty.

Clouds sailing lonely changing shapes over our heads

With the gentle breeze as if played with piano of rhapsody

We are the only two to feel the presence of omnipresent god

That accompanies us to decide the journey of rest life.

3. THE SEASON OF LOVE

Every season a season of love
Summer of life full of mirth
Rainy day the season of birth
Winter provokes love and lust
Something gained if something lost
Autumn the seasons of tenderness
Makes life easier for happiness
Life enlivens in the season of spring
Come to light the new siblings.

4. MY FATHER

One who can fight against the God?
When I am hurt or injured
To get quick recovery assured in freshness
He is none other than my father, his vastness.
One who loves in disguise?
In silence blesses me to rise
With more power in shape, size and shrewdness
He is none other than my father, his highness.
One can provide me everything unconditional
Who wishes me to be rational, social
Makes himself happy with my happiness
He is none other than my father, his sacredness.
One who always likes my dislikes and ugliness
Stealthily moulds my goodness
Understands me and my willingness
He is none other than my father, his greatness.

5. DOING NO MISTAKES

Mistakes are not done rather happen unconscious
Some mistakes under subconscious are rigorous
But mistakes under conscious are sternly noxious
Embrace each mistake, a lesson too precious.
Mistakes are necessities to enrich each part of life
Consciousness of doing no mistakes
Is a great mistake to leave something incorrigible
Wrong cannot be right unless and until comprehensible.
Man of no mistakes is likely to be omniscient or a lunatic
No person under the sun born with squeaky clean
Mistakes only pave the way, experience to glean
And experiences vouchsafe practical knowledge.

6. BETTER DAYS

Better days never come better for a hater

Days are neither sweet nor bitter in the language of a poetaster

It is our thoughts in which can shelter

Both are same if you filter or flatter in the voice of a songster

The ways you see through gutter not always batter.

Days are better only when battered on the anvil of a tester

Emerged through dust and moisture, mud and water

Enlightened by the thunderbolt and black clouds glitter

Whacked by the master blaster spinner or a batter.

Bitter days repeatedly test patience and diligence

Read your mind, nature, behavior and intelligence

Drench in the lake of torture, gloom and penitence

Making everything convenient for better day's resilience.

Better days come with the twittering of little birds

In the reconciliation of lovers with a resolute fresh start

Loving, caring and sharing each other by heart

Better days can never be apart.

7. LOVE TIME

Time is not as limpid as fluid water

Not as squishy as satiny butter

Not as adamantine as stiff iron

But time is everything for aeon.

No fire burns, no rain drenches, no snow freezes

Time is everywhere, sometimes swells, sometimes squeezes

As singers voice more mellifluous when comes through musical instruments

A crevice is enough for time to pass through ailments.

Keep on running after time not after money

Time will offer you pure love, peace and harmony

No doubt you can neither she nor touch time

But time beholds you, passes you without waiting.

Love time by heart and be like time

Everyday will be your valentine.

8. GOOD THINGS TAKE TIME

Success doesn't come in a day
A matter of lenience and toil
No need to stay in turmoil
Waiting doesn't let you recoil.
A nine month's travail
Of a mother, ultimately hail
A neonate baby to quell
Fright of uncertainty, fail.
Good things filter the best
Out of all odds and muck
Each moment to face a test
Making friends with soil and rock.
Delay is not injurious in any way
Refinement takes place to sway
Rainbow peeps through clouds
Gold flares after one mould.
It takes time to better the better
Spring turns up only after winter
Fetter not you in the chains of haste
Don't let the good to be waste.

9. WHAT YOU GIVE COMES BACK TO YOU

Human beings truly a resource

Being expert in a discipline in due course

Varieties of slabs seen among the people

Rich-poor, high- low, white-black, common-uncommon

Friends-foes, peon-officer, thieves-police, nurse- surgeon.

Some are noble givers, some are only receivers

Some are simply helpers, some are just beholders

Some are volunteers, some are scapegoats and mongers.

You are in you everything one may see in difference

The same person having many fold features with versatility

Some possessed, we believe, of divine creativity

Some are great by birth, some are with inborn quality.

Some busy for nothing, some busy for something meaningful

Whatever you do or give will nourish your future

There's no denying the fact that the present is treasure

Be sure, as per actions, in return you will either be gainer or looser.

Choice is yours to make up your mind

Love and to be loved reciprocal of its kind

The world is sufficient enough to pay what you need

If you care of others, somebody in disguise will take your heed.

10. ONE WHO FALLS CAN RISE

Poison or nector never known untill is tasted
So is curry saulty or watery
What you see is not always true to be trusted
Something lies behind the story.
Defeat is not a defeat a step towards bravery
Failure is not a failure an attempt to regain victory
Flop and foibles in love make you stronger to be a true lover
A new beginning starts to hover.
Gold gleams only after being burnt and battered
New twigs grow only after the old ones snicked
The sun rises in the east when it sets in the west
A child falls many a time before it rises to stand.
One who falls again and again can rise to perfections
Falling and failing corrects and makes one bold
To balance oneself with actions and reactions
Finally learns and teaches how to stand and uphold.
Never, never think of rising without falling into sorrow
How can you pluck fruits without sowing seeds in the furrow?
The more you fall, the more you rise to survive
Somewhere you have to revolt, something to revive.

11. LET'S MAKE LIFE MEANINGFUL

Believed that human life is the fruit of myriad meditation

Salvation from beasts, the result of emancipation

One time offer gifted by the loving Almighty

The foremost and most loveable form of incarnation.

Human life has several meanings to define

The more you analyze the more it will be pristine

All traits He bestow upon humans to make life meaningful

And hopes the best from us with living purposeful.

He has made some artists, poet, singer and writer

Some as makers, builders, philosopher and orator

Brain to capture, heart to rapture, hands to feed unconditional

Mind to judge, emotions to indulge in goodness affordable.

Some of us, more or less, are something useful

Some have charismatic quality to impress excciteful

Some have simplicity to win the heart of many

Some have greatness to reshape the society with harmony.

Life is stored with plenty of synonyms, antonyms, homonym and acronym as well

Read it, listen it before speaking or writing and live well

Life is the combination of loss and gain, pain and pleasure, heaven and hell

Then duty is yours to choose the right option to peacefully dwell.

12. BE MY VALENTINE

Be my valentine I promise I shall be yours
All wishes I fulfill be sure
The sunrise and sunset will be ours to decorate
All time all places to accommodate
Where you can no more suffocate
Everything everywhere we can emulate.
The night will be too longer to see the sweet dreams
Days will be shorter for us to greet with bream
Our love together will make a utopia to reside
Where no current will flow with ebb and tide
A new paradise emerges for us to hide
Where we only the first and last couple inside.
Be my valentine I assure everything pristine
We will be at cloud nine
When I shall yours and you will be mine
We will make our own world of love that will shine
The rest will be very fine.
Nothing to hinder, nothing to sender us to join lifetime.
O valentine, be my valentine dear
Let the mankind remember us here.

13. A LETTER TO THE ALMIGHTY

O omnipresent why so silent

Omniscient you are but acquiescent

Let me know it's thy lenience or indifference

If time pushes you in the dungeon of silence

May you send an invisible superman?

To subdue the forces of worldwide violence.

At least my Lord in your absence.

O Almighty, give all your might to do the right

In disguise over day and night

Dress him in the attire of invisibility

Equip him with the indiscernible arms of fire, air, water in plenty

Bless him with nonviolent tools of equality, fraternity

Bestow upon him the grace of commitment and integrity

Speechless speech to mesmerize the mass of vulnerability.

O shapeless, untouched and unseen mighty power

Before your feet let me put forth my prayer

Thou are the anchor, controller and center

But you are felt helter-skelter

Why not send your invisible character

When the dishonest drench the world with flood of corruption

The whole mankind needs your interruptions.

14. LIFE IS A BOAT

Life is a boat

Every day it is to float

On the surface water of society

And we are mere boatmen, rowing is our duty

Early in the morning it starts its journey

Rests in the evening passing through cacophony.

Chances are there the boat may dash against any rock

May a little drop of water gush to the crevice of the deck

Be cautious lest the oar should slip from your hand.

Unwanted waves might come with force

And gets it destroyed before reaching the shore

Inevitable are the mishaps at any time approach without any call

Sometimes the reasons of one's downfall.

Life is a boat

And we are mere boatmen

But stop shrinking you, try again

The light house stands ahead to steer the direction.

15. SOMETHING THAT.....

Something that hurts not always painful
What you avoid can make life meaningful
Teaches a great lesson making one resourceful
Somebody who hates you never hates you
He is under compulsion to act that is not what you see
In disguise he heartily loves you
Something that praises you not always meaningful
Behind the curtain hides someone harmful
Something that pleases you not always mirthful
Something that saddens you not always doleful.

16. LET WORDS BE USEFUL

Words are yours but effect or affect others more and more
Some hurt, some cut with sore
Some allure by heart and soul
Like a magnate sticks to the nearby iron ore.
Words flowing from mouth work as sweets to please
The same may often come, poison to release
The way you speak matters a lot whether to seize or tease
Decision left to you how it can be employed.
Words are meaningful that can mean various ways to define
Words are powerful that can fill the blank of life to refine
Words are harmful that can break heart to resign
The speakers must know beforehand how to design.
Words as wizards hypnotize many a mind
Make one yield in something to rescind
What no sages or peers can do for ages
Within a winking of eye it raises to blaze.

17. EVERY PAIN TEACHES A LESSON

When there's life, there's plenty of emotions, sentiments

Five senses together build life

Each sense gets hurt when faces a test to perceive the taste

Hot or cold, salty or watery, sweet or sour, the worst or the best.

Pain of hunger saves every bit of bread from wastage

A hungry man knows the proper value of shortage

Both sweet and sour can grab the same weightage

Thus a painful life always takes an extra mileage.

Pain of poverty every day and night makes a resolution

Continuously and continually keeps life's journey on with concentration

He makes use of nature's gift staying tuned to reverberation

Before his fearless commitment acquiesces all risky and deadly weapons.

Life gets renewed and refreshed with the pain of hardships or adversity

A new world of newness takes birth experiencing maturity

Pillared by unimagining faith and trust casting the roof of integrity

Stands as a legendary heritage of wonders replete with divinity.

Pain of failure so bitter that can plaster the nudity with a paste

Colored by countless chances to have finishing with zest

Marvels the previous, amazing sophistication in all respect crest

To offer whole world the pellucid day light the mighty sun has to set in the west.

Have a warm hug; every pain leaves a life-making lesson

Equip yourself with this weapon of semons to unleash perfection.

18. MOTHER LANGUAGE DAY

Human's first language
That is mother language
Learned without usage
Every nation's heritage.
No teacher is required
Automatically acquired
What a language it is
In love, affection enriched.
Gives human identification
Geographically demarcation
Linguistically categorization
Owning speciality in segregation.
Language of emotions
Heartfelt expression
Weapon of humanization
Lifelong reverberation.
A day of appreciations
Committed to utilization
Shows us destination
Language of close relation.
A day of taking solemn oath
For mother language growth
Freedom of communication
Needs no prior permission.

Language listens from mother
Enters into heart's chamber
No pain to ever remember
For her let's stand together.
One language one region
Abounds in culture, religion
Now soaring worldwide
The flight of mankind.
Now regional to national
National to international
To world language equal
Journey runs continual.
Live long mother tongue
Throng never can abandon
Separately inseparable
Mother and mother tongue.

19. SITUATIONS CHANGE A MAN

Human being such a sibling naturally growing
Becomes a beast while, in forest, staying
In society among the fellows a social being, among the sages a moral
being
Somewhere wild somewhere mild, amazing.
Change is the process of Nature to nurture creation thriving.
Sometimes blind in spite of having eyes to espy
Stands dumb even if gifted with a mouth to convey
Lacks the power of hearing when someone is grieving
Jeopardized to extend helping hands to those seeking
A person changes as to place, position or situation quite taxing.
A rickshaw puller can speak English fluently
Without visiting any boarding school consistently
Or without learning grammar and usages perfectly
Has been staying in English spoken environment since genesis
Often not possible for a higher degree holder to accomplish.
Helpless is many a man going against the opposite direction
Record of history seen break civilization after civilization
Time under situation forced to change the regulations
However raises an uphill task to finish with determinations
No matter healthy or unhealthy a situation.

20. PAINTING

Picture drawn by imagination
Colored by emotions
Painted by devotion
Reality reflects heart's reverberation
More lively than life
More beautiful than admiration
Can change my conception
Drag me out from hallucination.
Eyes gazed at her
Ears hark only her
Face sticked by miring in image
Fluttering round the beholder for ages
Trapped in mind's cage.

21. ENEMIES ARE ALSO FRIENDS

Be grateful to your enemies for remembering to hate

You are the number one in the list of target

No sooner do they get a chance than start exploring weakness

To topple the fort of your name, fame and richness

Are not they reasons to rise in you the sun of awareness?

Be thankful you have enemies to plant the seeds of thorns on your way

Leaving the one filled with flowers of tenderness towards goals doorway.

Sweet enemies and bitter friends equally as deadly as poison

But in camouflage warn us to remain aloof from dungeon.

Enemies are like darkness dense, gloomy and gelid to light on.

True is the common saying 'barking dogs never bite'

Mighty sun for long time, black clouds can never hide

Flee away after leaving some lessons to mankind

Enemies roar like thunder, come like gusty wind and run away

Becoming powerless after a while and melt away.

Keep in mind enemies are also friends to guide us in disguise

Urging us to follow up the right path in right time to surmise

Be truthful, honest and fair to your enemies to defeat unhurt

Let's live with them and grow as lotus in water untouched

Enemies and friends inseparable flames residing in the same heart.

22. POETRY VS WOMAN

Without love neither poetry nor woman well understood
Unfathomable is the depth limitless face in hood
Interminable source, imperceptible, uninterrupted force
Takes much time to be illustrated for those who don't reinforce
Both poetry and woman are lovers of love to be loved.
One an admirer of dazzling ornaments of winking pearl
The other of figure of speech- similes or metaphor
Unparalleled, unquestionable and incomparable sapphires
The ogle in beauty, the naked serenity makes us decipher
Both look gorgeous when dressed in sparkling apparel.
Painted by the pigment of simply shyness
Tinted by the hue of virginity and sacredness
Sometimes coyed in cares to be hugged in distress
Conquering the stress of exaggeration, the hidden veracity to trace
Very choosy, cozy well wishers are keenly impressed to grace.
Both are adequately creative and highly productive by nature
Pregnant in positivity, abundant in constructive actions to nurture
The pensive mood, the upset soul healing and deriving pleasure
At first sight with last impression throughout life in rapture
A choice for someone when an option for literature.

23. JOURNEY OF LOVE

A divine gift offered to humans with inception of birth
Then starts the journey of love to one's last breath
In some cases spreads the fragrance of love even after death
Journey of love continues with the journey of life.
Life lives on love that enriches depressed heart and soul
That unites mankind in the string of harmony and peace
That upholds the load of ensuing generations in bliss
The path of journey becomes glossy and flossy to accomplish
Let everybody mingle in the Journey of seraphic love
Whole-heartedly sacrificing own selfishness and greediness
With a promise to stand for each other in loneliness
Towards the destination of success filled with sacredness.
A new world of unity and fraternity will rise
Sowing the seeds of affection and compassion in every heart
To enlighten the path of destination
Each one a component of equality in the civilization.

24. FILIAL THANKFULNESS

Thankful to those who cares me without condition
Loyal to me in my worst tough and rough situation
Believe in me with hundred percent confidences
Support my positive thoughts and self relience .
Thankful to those who still sustain the divine humanity
Dreaming of reshaping the destiny of future society
Abide by the ethics and values that guides morality
Share a few words that work as ointment in adversity.
Thankful to those who understand themselves and others
Love one's personality and character remain immortal forever
Stay away from malafide intention to surpass perfection
Ready to extend helping hands during life's superannuation.
Thankful to those who bring us to see the light
Make us stand, speak and walk on the path right
The present our conspicuous treasure that lives with us delight
Respecting the past that teaches, stimulates and excites.

25. EVERYBODY HAS OWN SPECIALITY

All are not equal in a broader sense

In between you and me there's is a fence

But worry not about that distance

Everybody has his own specialist and significance.

Each specialty is meaningful widens the scope of intelligence.

More or less in one way or the other

Different we are, still lucky enough to stand together

What makes us equal above and over all is humanity

That's only our identity working for solidarity and equality.

Love and respect to each other our morality

Feel and understand to one another our maturity

Sharing and caring come from our magnanimity

Can we find all these in one personality?

Small is useful, black is beautiful, agree or disagree

A bard can never stop crooning whether captivated or free

No one becomes great or small in giving thanks or feeling sorry

But heart changes to break the record of history.

26. HANKER NOT AFTER BEAUTY

Beauty is black but everybody traces the track
What beguiles you may betray
If you wish, do hanker after traits
That will make you straight.
Beauty looks wonderfully colorful
Making, for a moment, everyone mirthful
None can ensure that it's not at all harmful
Something we are missing blissful.
Eyes get tempted, beauty befooles
Men of hollow cannot skedaddle
How long can exist a water babble?
Deep and dense color deeply dwindles.
Good manners make good character
And good character dashing personality
Beauty is fleeting, leaving one crestfallen
Yearn for the beauty of personality not to repent again.
Shimmering beauty one day loses its enticement
But inner beauty never disappoints excitement
The way you see matters a lot to define its sanctity
Where lies ugliness, where pristine beauty.

27. CHOOSING A DIFFERENT PATH

One ambition irreversible for competition

But umpteen ways ahead to destination

Path followed one after the other becomes specified and conspicuous

Choosing a different path outright inconspicuous.

Choosing a different path undoubtedly strenuous but not infeasible

Takes longer time and toil to accomplish the task incorrigible

Makes the travellers sanguine of maximum triumph unbelievable.

Different path, from all others, makes different

Be different to make difference graced by Omnipresent

When nobody is there with you or none to like you

God is with you as He wants you become special in lieu.

To be different is risky but the end is full of ecstasy

Sleeping in the bed of luxury is the beginning of misery

Adversity and sorrows teach how to cope with situation

Heart swings in the ripples of reverberation.

28. BAD TIMES NEVER LAST LONG

Dark clouds of bad times rumble

In fright many a heart tremble

Some chicken hearts mildly topple

After a sojourn it may take farewell humble.

Bad times never last long

Worry not too much, dear throng.

As it comes so does it go away?

Leaving some bitter memories

Somewhere for some as calories

Depressed life it can deeply enrich

Bad times never last long

Listen to the rhythm of Nature's song.

29. WORLD WRITERS DAY

Writers are Social Workers.
A day of golden opportunity to remember the world writers
With unfathomable love, affection, respect and homage for their contribution
Writers of the world are dreamers of the better world in gratification
Over day and night sacrificing own time and labour to explore
For welfare of the generations to come with novel lore
Reader of the world writers before they are writers
Leaving the common world to become universal fighters
Dedicated to reshape the whole world brighter
Workers of society promoted to nation and then the universe
Remolding every disorder of the world with fair purpose
Inner truth they can disclose before the humanity
Tilling the barren land of ignorance to harvest fertility
Evergreen are their vegetables of creativity
Rear the whole world with perpetual profound wisdom
Diamond forever sparkling even after demise
Assuage the appetite of inquisitiveness in disguise
Yearning for the honour and privilege of the race to rise
My great salute to the writers of the world today and tomorrow
For their imperishable service to the society to grow.
May you live long writers guiding the people's destination?
You are the real fighters to unleash pure perfection.

30. WRITERS ARE REFORMERS

Think not writers are ordinary persons
In one sense ordinary as they are humans
But extraordinary personality they possess as writers
Enlighten the whole world as the empyrean lighters.
Remolding the old into new in thoughts and actions
As the harbingers of transition and reformations
Writing with thoughts provoking and prudence deserve illustration
Customs, traditions, habits, culture and religion get renewed
In the hands of writer-reformers enthusiastic and shrewd.
Garnering the best from the dustbin of each corner of society
To scour the filth of narrowness scattered here and there in the locality
For days and nights they keep them busy deploying resourceful acuity
In the realm of every aspect of human life.
Love for near and dear, bent for society, nation and proclivity for world community
Lead them on the way of refinement and commitment with integrity
Every day brings a clarion call making them sagacious
Let's cherish their contributions to know how precious for us.

31. SCARY WAR

O humans, are you really human kind
Coming from the world of lovely mankind?
In the name of peace running after power
The root cause of catastrophic war.
O, humans are you really educated to change
Or so called savage to take revenge?
Because you read and write what is written
To exploit the innocent illiterate rustic from a village.
O humans are you really cultured, modern?
From greenness to grayness you are striving to transform
Don't think so as you are least concerned
Like a heartless stone remain untrodden.
O humans are you really free or afraid of other's freedom ?
Conqueror of inhumanity to widen the vast kingdom.
Taking pleasure to push the rivals into the thralldom
But war will never sort out your conundrum
For which you are devastating the eternal world of wisdom.

32. IF YOU WANT PEACE

Stop pretending yourself to be always right
Because you may be wrong for someone
Nothing in the world is correct or perfect
Be sanguine of maximum positivity, no suspect.
Stop welding power upon anyone known or unknown
Power seekers are smugglers of humanity as don
Bad times come to any might under the sun
Anything or anybody ascends or descends in their turn.
Stop comparing others as all are not equal
Inner conflicts start reigning over your soul
When friends turn to enemies the fair or the foul
You are the reason of sorrows or happiness to ghoul
Stop worrying about what you lose or gain
Loss or gain two sides of the same coin
No denying the fact that there's pain in joy and joy in pain
One-sidedness topples down the palace of dreams golden.
Stop cheating yourself to cheat others for your benefit
Time is witnessing to punish the culprit
Expect not more than what you are or you have
Excess avarice injurious to your future, you cannot save.

33. LIFE NEVER STOPS TEACHING

Flowers bloom before they fade

The sun rises before it sets

Water bubble beautifies before it melts away

All things are good before going astray

Life teaches before it ends.

Each moment of life a priceless gift

Heart enlivens in the swirling ripples, stage to shift

Train of life delays but makes up time to arrive at the platform

Each step of life lavishes a ladder to climb.

Life never stops teaching the one who needs

So never stop learning a complete potion to feed

The more one learns, more he teaches how to take heed

Of unconscious belief, emotions and traumas to get rid.

34. HAPPY HOLI, 2022

Hearty welcome to happy holi
A festival of colours, quite holy
People forget enmity, envy, and anger
Pregnant with love and compassion for keeping in touch
Yearly festival of mankind, rapture to dispatch.
Happy and make others happy
Oscillating in the stage of joy
Lament not on the past that is absent
Inhale the fragrance of present.
Happy holi come fresh
One and all to refresh
Grace, embrace and impress
Malafide intentions to suppress.

35. WHAT DO YOU DREAM

How different the bygone world of innocence and simplicity

From the present world of sophistication and anxiety

Immeasurable the gap of two generations

One the earth replete with fertility, productivity and integrity

The other the limitless sky of hollow, vacuum and fertility.

Then time when flowers of divinity bloomed with fragrance of frankness

Life lived in tiny the hut of happiness with truthfulness

When the elders showered upon the younger's the stream of heartfelt blessings and kindness

Distilled was water, fresh was water and thus conducive the habitat for existence.

When all difficulties melt away like a piece of snowflake

Togetherness simplified the problems intricate and complicated

A crowd of members having nothing but stayed safe and blessed

What they got back free of cost is peace and joy.

A dim light of candle enlightened the dense darkness to have sound sleep

When no fear of theft, robbery, suspect, and mockery to slip

Really the bygone days were everything in nothing

But the present is nothing in everything.

36. LEARN FROM EVERYONE

Everyone is created by the same Creator

With a purpose less or more, sweet or bitter

Ways of journeys different but to the goal one

Follow no one, but learn from everyone.

Everyone travels on his own way of life

Liked by some, but disliked by many

Depending upon their own choice as per mindset

Because all are not equally blessed to target.

Everyone not endowed with everything he wants

He is not enough to hold all sources

As a river requires to take away the other wishes to mingle with sea

One seeks others to fulfill the basic needs in glee.

Everyone is born with an inherent speciality

When the other may lack of such opportunity

Complementary to each other for any fulfillment.

37. FATHER

A man of belief who never deceives
Without any clues he perceives
A source of unfinished strength and motivation
An undefeated warrior in the battlefield of resolution
He is the solution, A man of joy and happiness soaring in the azure of revolution
He is the man who swallows the poison of sorrows and suffering
Morn to night sips the sweat of toil and turmoil without caring
He makes the mountain move and run
For his daughter and son
He is the narration.
He is the superhero a man of fearlessness
He the moon among the stars to twinkle in darkness
A man of silence who makes me speak in vividness
He is the man who can dry the water of ocean
Who can tear down the blanket of hallucination?
He is superb creation.
Father is a father of father
He is the sun who neither rises in the east nor sets in the West
Incessantly constant standing for the rest
In the mundane realm he is the best.
He is someone's dreams, someone's faith and confidence
He is the man who makes love grow fair in credence
Relationship to care in perseverance
He is the man of reverence.

38. MY DREAMS

Life bloomed with the flowers of dreams
Enriches one with ingredients that beams
My dreams my food for my appetite
Show me the path always right.
Dreams are doorway to destination
Facing both fantasy and reality
Driving away the force of hallucination
Makes me a man of creativity.
Dreams are the ladders to possibility
Stepping one by one steps of .positivity
Makes me feel the taste of nobility
That brightens my sensibility.
Dreams are seen to set the goal
Like gum it closes life's hole
Enchanting the divinity of soul
Life is set with dreams as a whole.
To me my dreams are all in all to make me rich in humanity
Maker, builder, motivator to bring equality and equity
Revitalizer, changer, ranger to establish fraternity
My dreams are my strength to stand for solidarity.

39. HAPPINESS LIES IN NOTHINGNESS

Happiness a state of mind lying within
No materials, no property yields in
No possessions buy or sell in market
Cannot captivate inside your pocket.
Minimum accumulations, maximum gratification
Maximum desires minimum satisfaction
Life with anything excess invites own destruction
The more one flies high, more he falls.
The best way to seek happiness
Habit of staying in nothingness
Keeping yourself at what you are
From heaven happiness will shower.
Sacrifice, adjustment and compromise
For seeking happiness blessings in disguise
Choice and option in your hands to finalize.

40. MY FATHER

One who can fight against the God
When I am hurt or injured
To get quick recovery assured in freshness
He is none other than my father, his vastness.
One who loves in disguise
In silence blesses me to rise
With more power in shape, size and shrewdness
He is none other than my father, his highness.
One can provide me everything unconditional
Who wishes me to be rational, social?
Makes himself happy with my happiness
He is none other than my father, his sacredness.
One who always likes my dislikes and ugliness
Stealthily moulds my goodness
Understands me and my willingness
He is none other than my father, his greatness.

41. WEDDING

Wedding Weds Two Souls
Part Becomes Whole
Welding worries and nostalgia
Often works more than panacea.
Ending the end of depression
Passing of age closes tension
Union of views and opinions
Intermingles in juxtaposition.
Over years of awaited desires
Flaming in the oven of flairs
Blazes with fun and social fairs
A promise, each other to care
A bond of love and affection
Where there's no pretension
Flicker of hope bonds together
Both of them free in al weather.
Two poles well in errection
Able to keep on institution
For forthcoming generation
A belief never faces extinction.

42. TIME

I know I can't touch you
How can I seize you?
Nobody run after you
How can I reach you.
Still have an earnest
Request for my sweetest
Whom I can understand
Let night be sleepless
When I can embrace
Her to adorn fullest
Let me love her full
Let Night close her eyes
Till we measure each other
The shape and size
Depth of emotions
To mingle the ebb and tide
Lying hidden behind
Taking the flow of likes and dislikes
Together we can do
Keeping on recreating
Something special for you.

43. BEAUTY

Everybody tempted, captivated in your refulgence
Poet's pen ripples in words in your elegance
Bees start flutterting round you to kiss the rosy lips
Eyes of the beholders dazzled promises to keep.
Thou are symphony of rhymes, magic, music, melody to whisper
Without light you shimmer, new thoughts and ideas prosper
Thy genesis echoes all round to energise the disheartened viewers
What a charisma you have that makes one and all super.
No humans who don't hanker after you to embrace
No rivals remain silent to bet him or her to win you in the race
After you the whole world is his who is really blessed
In euphoria many a man ready everything to replace.
Thou are the monsoon emerge in time and pass away
Like thunder you come and flood the earth and flee away
Everybody swirls in the whirls of hallucination
After your sovereign reign of inclination and mesmeric intoxication.
O, beauty, much addressed as queen, sweetheart or dream girl
How quickly you magnetize the lovers like poetic pearl
But the way you come, you go away out of sight
How forlorn, what a Nature's creation, you go out of mind. !!!

44. BANYAN TREE

Standing beside the road at the edge of village
Witnesses the passerby's passing in and out
Mirrors the pain and pleasure of villagers
Every mood engraved on its chest.
Shade of chili and cooling air refresher
Fans the rivulet of sweat under swinging leaves
Taking the booster doze of ease delighted to rush the firm
Overtime of hardships diluted under her serene lap.
Shelter of myriads lives breathing in tha air of tranquility
Breathing out the sigh of deep, dense adversity
Feeling rapturous even though the pensiveness reigns over anxiety.
Abode of deities, fairies and angels the inhabitants believe
At the outset accompanying her gracious blessings some start their
journey
Some bowing their heads before the mother banyan tree
Having abundance faith and trust for the victory over cacophony.
Over decades of patience and stamina stands for benevolence
Wishing the best of luck to her returnee in silence
Never allows the cruel sun, naughty rain through her canopy of density
and openness
To hurt any of her loving sojourners in loneliness.

45. POETRY IS A DEAL OF JOY, PAIN AND WONDER.

Poetry blooms in the flowery garden of my heart

With resplendent colors of feelings and emotions

Some deep, some light and some dim even in blink

Word pictures so painted, crafted seeming lively to wink.

The more rapturous in one's fulfillment and pleasure

Likewise more depressed, dolorous in other's torture

Bcoz committed is poetry to deal twin symphony of treasure

Equally with poetic justice, how wondrous to measure.

Poetry croons the song of both join and pain

Creating the citadel of sun and rain

Exploring the truth in lies and lies in truth

Perceives a sense of pain in joy and joy in pain.

46. POETRY THIEF

Poetry is not a matter of competition to gain promotion

It is heart's inner self presentation of emotions

No one can write better in comparison

No poetry penned under compulsion.

It is a matter of composition not a game to play

Creativity never blesses anybody who wants to pay

So foolish to be a poet plagiarizing other's ink to say

By doing so one is letting humanity go astray.

God has not made humans equally so far as talent or luck is concerned

Never strive to compare with any other person

Gifted with His grace, divinity and imagination

One can never quench his thirst dreaming mirage of hallucination.

O poetry thief, better to die than to show your false pride

Thou are the omen of insensibility, you can't hide

Keep silence and stay far from the madding crowd

No rains shower cats and dogs from roaring clouds.

Poetry thief either a drinker or a smuggler of letters

With borrowed words how long he twitters.

47. FUN OF HOLI

A fest of colours reminding deep love of couple
Real lovers the worshipers of love divine and humble
Love is where Radha and Govind sway under the maple
In the core of heart, waves of love incessantly ripple.
Colours paint symphony of human feelings and emotions
Enriches the realm of humanity with affection and compassion
Colours reflect the portrait of actions and reactions
Colours of love never fade in rains or in sun.

48. SMILING FACE

Everybody has a face to look at
Ugly or beautiful no matter
But a smiling face can attract
Removing strife pleases better
It mirrors pleasure and positivity
Erases the scars of worries and anxiety
That can enrich a mind of futility
A talisman to drive away evils of negativity
Smiling face a natural cosmetic
So alluring and hypnotic
Mesmerizes many a man sadistic
Enables to remain full time active.
It hopefully makes a man mirthful
An ocean of inspiration needful
Panacea to all disorder corrigible
Nothing remains fearful or harmful.
A gift of divinity to human nature
Just have a smiling to rapture
Many more free to culture
Imparts how to survive a culture.

49. A POET?

Common a man, uncommon his contribution
Unacknowledged a legislator, acknowledged his laws for humanization
A dreamer of golden future, a preserver of culture
A person of distant vision, a passionate literature.
God gifted man with the power of sixth sense
Can see in the third eye what others cannot sense
Invisible social worker toiling for reformation
Meditation his food, humanity his religion, inking his passion.
Simply a cultivator ploughing the land of creation
Endures all hardships to harvest the crops of marvel fruition
Imperishable his wealth, unending source in distribution
Like a honey bee garners honey even from virulent blossoms.
A searcher of novelty, discoverer of past, inventor of tomorrow
Treasures the present to frame the ensuing generations to glow
In the storm of follies and foibles appears as rainbow.
Letting the lamp of hope, credence to guide the hollow.

50. WOMAN - THE CREATOR

A woman common to the world
But uncommon beyond imagination
Mother a creator more than a Creator
Who always takes pain and risks to shoulder?
Mother is not just a lady to look after family and home
Laying the foundation of love and affection
Over the pillars of patience, endurance and commitment
Builds the citadel of understanding, compromise and adjustment.
An undefeated soldier and lifelong warrior to promise the safety
In no situation can allow any enemy of quarrel and animosity?
To devide her creation, to break the divine relation
She is the only one who likes the likes and dislikes of children.
She can do anything for her creation at the cost of life
Every day she can sip the water of human strife.

51. A PARENT'S LOVE

Unconditional as free as natural resources
Incomparable, things become pale before her face
Unquestionable is his way of caring and sharing
Unfathomable depth of love and affection
Indescribable the story remains untold for generations
Indestructible under the sun over the years of reflections
As limpid as water mirroring heartfelt magnanimity
As sweet as honey and as holy as divinity
As sparkling as diamond forever to allure
Tremendous her vigour and valour
Panacea to all mental and physical ailments of children
Reshapes the destiny of sons and daughters.

52. A FESTIVAL OF UNITY

Puri, a district of Odisha, the abode of the lord Jagannath

Grateful to Him for His wish to reside in Shree Mandir (temple)

Where assembled devotees from local and abroad

During the time of the Car Festival

A festival of unity.

When people forget their caste creed and religion

Forget their name, fame place and position

When all are only the fiends having one ambition

Emancipation from the selfish action

Forever salvation sustaining humanity

The festival of fraternity.

The festival of majestic assemblage

With aesthetic beauty of nature and culture intermingled

Mesmerizing the worldwide maniacs

The clouds of diversity melt away at the advent of Trinity

The whole world seems to be a family of equity abd equality.

53. LOVE

Love seeks no explanation

It needs action

Love doesn't speak

But understands beyond doubt

Love doesn't compare

Welcomes all irrespective of caste, creed and religion

Reciprocal in sharing and caring

Melts away the unrequited love poison.

54. LET LIFE LIVE

Life so meaningful to make it useful
Anyone can interpret anyway suitable
Place, person or time adds synonyms and antonyms
Life is a vast dictionary compiled with unlimited usages and vocabulary.
Everyday a life turns up with a new beginning
Facing ups and downs during travelling
Interference, interruptions often tears myriads hearts
Experiencing bitter truth of life that deeply imparts.
Life is neither defeat nor victory rather a mixture of two in one
Anybody balancing seems to be successful person
To lose is not to gain but a chance to render something the best
But loss of life extinguishes the light of hope.
O humans of super creation let life live
No matter whether you perceive or deceive
What matters is life a great lesson to teach
Everyday more or less it enriches the pinnacles to reach.

55. EASY OR DIFFICULT THINGS

Easy to hate, difficult to love

Insult not to consult.

Easy to break, difficult to make

Making excuses seems fake.

Easy to make a lie, difficult to speak the truth

Road to success is not always smooth.

Easy to pass comments, difficult to pass knowledge

Life an unfathomable source to encourage.

Easy to fall in the well of negativity, difficult to float in the clouds of positivity

Without experience no one obtain full maturity.

Easy to conspire, difficult to admire

Life is replete with fuel and fire.

Easy to vacate, difficult to accumulate

Both bad and good things in one way or the other stimulate.

Easy things are not always right to accept

Right things are not easy to direct precept.

Difficult Things differently decorate life with fertility

Choice is yours to opt for the exploration of reality.

56. MAKING SUICIDE

Suicide neither a solution nor a suggestion
Rather an instance of dehumanization
Life is not yours but someone's gift to you
Embrace it, love it, and respect it too.
Suicide an unrepairable loss to generations
A heinous crime
No relatives stay at cloud nine
Making suicide not your birth right.
Don't take it as an easy weapon
That murders your life
Nobody or nothing under the sun
Except you, can wash away your strife.

57. YOU ONLY FAIL IF YOU QUIT

An action a process of efforts and execution
Incessant exploitation of continuation
Only criteria employed for possible acquisition
Incompleteness persists on quitting application
Let fear of failure flee away far in you introspection.
Regularizations with patience make things easier
Heart ripples in pleasure
Winning over uncertainty and complications
Flow of failure faints and fades in the world of operations
Final round is yours to explore the limitations.
Focus on one begets millionaire
Its reverse makes a man nugatory
Adherence to one is better than multipliers
Unsteadiness in words, thoughts or actions quite unfair
That topples down the tower of expectations in air
Leave not what once set up till you conquer.

58. CAMOUFLAGE

An art imparts a lot
Painted pictures open one's lot
Still hidden something
A technique to conquer.
A wise man's cunningness reshapes credence
A lion's witty tricks baffles some innocence
How can it be meant an ugly appearance?
Better to say a gifted nature of adroitness.
A source of making one's livelihood
For others shapes and saves destiny
Someone is victimized, some makes identity
What a strange creativity!

59. A FATHER NEVER DIES

The most worthy word in dictionary
Father lovely, lively well articulated, a treasury
Lies in the memory of generation's gallery
Can you be defined in a word, or in a sentence?
Or in an essay, novel, drama and poetry?
It is you who offered me the pen that inks today
It is you who held my hand that serves everyday
It is you who showed the path that reaches my destination
It is you who still lives in me to guide the right direction.
Father is not a person rather an institution
Father is never dead in his creation
Father is not a problem but a solution
He is not an ordinary man rather uncommon potion.
A father never dies for his sons and daughters
In rain, sun or winter he always makes shades of shelters
O father, I am nothing but your cherished contribution
Bless me to be a good father needless to mention.

60. HAPPINESS

Happiness a state of mind lying within
No materials, no property yields in
No possessions buy or sell in market
Cannot captivate inside your pocket.
Minimum accumulations, maximum gratification
Maximum desires minimum satisfaction
Life with anything excess invites own destruction
The more one flies high, more he falls.
The best way to seek happiness
Habit of staying in nothingness
Keeping yourself at what you are
From heaven happiness will shower.
Sacrifice, adjustment and compromise
For seeking happiness blessings in disguise
Choice and option in your hands to finalize.

61. THE PATH WE CHOOSE

Choosing a path is not easy
One must be choosy being crazy
Paths ahead full of diversions
The right one is uncertain
But we are compelled to obtain
One that is unknown
But making journey till last
Matters a lot nobody can forecast
No path is easy as one wishes
We have to make easier as to accomplish
Patience and perseverance together
Stands for those who love duty
Whichever path is taken further
If furnished with integrity
Then no chances of futility
One definitely able to gather
All ease and comfort anywhere
If he loves the path forever.

62. THOUGHTS

Nature reshapes destiny
Of things, creatures massive or tiny
Regenerating thoughts in mind's eye
Making the reality more than what others see
Nature whirls the tornado of Time
Winsome and gruesome sights chyme in rhyme
Crooning lullaby for sound sleep
Or else bewailing about corpses heap
Destroying is to remaking for a balance
And making for the glory robbed of with a passage of time.

63. MORE LEARNING MORE EARNING

The world is full of knowledge
Where life is a matter of learning
Which begets great earning
Thus earning relies on learning.
Life gets equipped in learning
The blank place of life needs filling
Little by little a day enough for acquiring
Everything is a source of learning.
Learning widens the scope of knowledge
Life should definitely take its mileage
Learning cultivates the land of heart and mind
In due time has much harvesting for mankind.
Learning turns pain to pleasure
Have learning a vast treasure
No one can easily measure
The depth of learning a revitalize.
Learning increases quality of acquisition
Quantity of calmness, humbleness
Decreasing the size of ignorance and weakness
Learning begets simplicity, humility and broadmindedness.

64. BEGINNING

O Beginning, thou are always hard
But I don't care
Because you can't stop me
As I am aware.
I know, You are an examiner
Always ready to examine
The test that makes me wins
Warming up every beginner.
O, Beginning, unquestionably an insightful trainer
Unbelievable thy trick certainly makes one gainer
Unforgettable the trials and tribulations
Without you, life can't move in any situations.
You are welcome my dear
Who wittily grab my fear?
Pushing me to the ocean of success
How can I forget you to embrace?
How can I forget to take your benign grace?

65. WORLD ENVIRONMENT DAY

We can do together if dedicated to create a better environment

O humans, come forward with your selfless commitments

Revenge not further for your own self fulfillment

Lest you should repent ove loss and predicaments

Do the needful day to day to nurture nature gaining her compliments.

Everywhere we live, move, flourish and achieve

Never ever deceive exploiting own place to leave

Vigorously believe freeing your heart and mind

Inner strength conceives to reshape the future in time

Respect, love, coddle the habitat as a mother to her children

O mankind be free and fair to live and let environment live

Neglect not to take care

Mother Earth who nourishes us

Even in our birth to death long journey prosperous

Neat and clean must we keep?

Together the dirt's we can sweep

Daily a day of bliss blesses us

Abundantly to make rapturous

Yet to fulfill the last wish wondrous.

66. WHY WOMEN SO BEAUTIFUL

Women are gifted with long hair dense and deep

On seeing the blackness the black bees weep

Open and glossy so eye catching to sweep

The dirts of distress from the corner of eyes and light to peep.

Women are graced with mellifluous voice

The depressed and deserted ears to rejoice

Cente of enticement encircled by circumference of only choice

Holding million minds of both fickle and grave stitches.

Women are enormously blessed with beguiling beauty

Spell of console and calm down to the naughty and the haughty

Power how to subdue the enemy and to regale the company

Convert the cacophony into life's symphony.

Women are made so beautiful to make society more beautiful

Stored with morale, fortitudes, all favour, flavour and ferver plentiful.

Enriched with potion, passion, patience, protection, love and peace to make life joyful

Supplemented and complemented with unique source of delight to make mankind peaceful.

67. WEALTH AND POVERTY

Everybody wants to be ofy

Nobody to be moocher

Nobody or nothing but actions can teach abundant

How to be affluent and makes one indigent.

Actions with devotion and integrity limits us to be materially wealthy

But makes mentally sharper, heightened in sensibility and physically healthy

Great and good actions alter attitudes, increase aptitudes

Stimulating the doers with multitude nobility and fortitude

Grandeur and fragrance of grand actions immortalizes souls

Slackness and negligence in assignments makes life barren whole.

What conspicuous is riches imparts how to be a doll dull

Decreasing the opulence of possession, ego and envy of tower fall

Poverty an empty vessel by nature needs filling

Affluence a deserted dustbin always seeks emptying.

Wealth is fire of desires that consumes humanity

Poverty a stream of thirst flows downwards to enrich the sea of humility.

Wealth teaches how to make a man pauper

Poverty teaches how to make a man richer.

68. ONE WHO LOVES

One who loves gets angry quickly
Because he/she loves very much
Who wants things to be good
In every stage of manhood.
One who loves hates too much first
To make love live up to the last
The more it stores more it blasts
For spreading aroma of triumph.
One who loves loses everything
To gain something something
Something becomes everything
And everything leaves nothing.
One who loves knows nothing
Sees nothing, listens to nothing
Sells nothing, buys nothing
Counts nothing, records everything.

69. YOU ARE MY INSPIRATION

Whoever you are, wherever you are
Whatever you are, whenever you are
Around me here and there, free and fair
Plants, animals, things, humans
No matters friends or foes
Bad or good, sweet or bitter, a small dose
Both are nature's charisma to repose
In any form, gender, caste and creed can never impose
All are the best creation
So you are my inspiration.
In everything I find education
Some pushes me in dungeon
Some drives me to perfection
Both are necessary requisition
To remould my imperfections
Life doesn't survive only with
Addition
Must is subtraction for purification
So you are all my inspiration.
Life grows amidst all likes and dislikes
Both help moving the chariot of life
Paves the way to flourish further
As life doesn't exist in loneliness
Better reshaped in togetherness

The earth where we live in not plain
Soil, water, stone, grass, trees and mountain
Streams, rivers, pits, mounds and drain
Together make the place habitat suitable
For everyone and everything to stay comfortable
In my pain and pleasure something useable
To breathe in peace and gratification
So, you are all my inspiration.

70. TRUE ROMANCE

Feel the absence
Seek the presence
Emotions intense
Can jump any fence.
Understand clues
Know the values
No specific milieu
You can allure.
Perceive the sense
As like as innocence
Love commonsense
As true as adolescence.
Tap the tender breast
Pinnacle you crest
Though not in haste
Delay is the best.
Yes, true romance
Life being reverberance
Stores in refulgence
Above and over the opulence.

71. HUMANITARIAN DAY

Humans are born humanitarian
Loving each other to comprehend
Liking each other to love and defend
Mending, fending being rituals to recommend.
Humans are born special creatures adorable
Differently distinguished, demandable
Sensible, rational and commendable
Conspicuously distinct in instinct and highly responsible.
Be positive to be constructive in thoughts and actions
Be sanguine of the best that lies in creations
Be a change to change yourself leading to perfections
Let each day be the humanitarian day for the sake of humanity
For spreading the blanket of love, peace and happiness over the world
community.
Both sweet and bitter words uttered by the same mouth
You yourself is the user to make up one's mind
Whether to accept or to rescind
Causing the cause of hurting and injuring in one hand
And caressing, hugging, making one smile in other hand.
Let the sun of Humanity shine in the east of humanization
Let each day for the humanitarian bloom
Of the humanitarian swipe away the waves of gloom
By the humanitarian unleash the world of boon.

72. COPYRIGHT OR PENRIGHT

Copyright or penright a writer's right
For owning no plagiarists should fight
A few innocent guys to delight as rite
However, caught in the trap of fright.
Creativity can never be available on rent
No part purchased or sold with full percent
As no water be segregated from milk to emphasize
No ingenuity be easily plagiarized to legalize.
Penright or copyright never saves its master's property
Unless and until one makes a career in humanity
Or a stringent action be taken against manipulation
Artistic world will be rusted away before germination.

73. INDEPENDENCE DAY

A day to salute tricolored flag of nation's essence deep and dense

For making us self dependent to sing the song of forefather's prudence.

A day to pay homage to the brave hearts who sacrificed their lives for
India's independence

Without whom it would not be possible to see the light of deliverance.

A day to commemorate the great lives of magnanimity and dedication

Whose actions paved the path of goodness leading to fruition?

A day to honour the revered luminaries who enlightened the dark of
nation

Let's respect the great soul with humble gratitude and appreciation

A day to take the follow up action for the betterment of future
generations

Who are waiting for their enrichment for perfection.

A day to feel being an Indian to avail the facilited rights offered by
constitution

Time to show warm gratefulness for its marvelous consideration.

A day to commit oneself for the good work of motherland and mother
language

An opportunity to serve the land, language and liberation

A day to promise for the safety and security of national property

Making our career in humanity for emphasizing love, peace and unity.

A day to celebrate the birthday of India's independence

Wit open heart having no feelings of discrimination and averance

With much mump and jubilation for being honoured with credence.

Chapter74

A slice of humanity everyday needs to be tasted

In the seraphic relation mankind wholly captivated

Sowing the seeds of love, affection and sympathy easily harvested

A gateway to reach the utopia of golden society without being invested.

Caring each other grows the plant of brotherhood

Drives away from the mind and heart the illusive mood

Let the resplendent flowers of transformation bloom

Melting away the snow of trauma and gloom.

Ability to share one another brings back love, peace and harmony

Crooning the carol of symphony amidst human's cacophony.

Let the gap be bridged by the embankment of brotherhood

To humanize mankind with the hymns of fraternity noble manhood.

Sharing pain and pleasure garners courage to stand

Helping in need invigorates to take your stand.

Doing and thinking good for others abounds in peace and prosperity

Maintaining and considering positive mind reshapes the destiny of humanity.

75. LOVE AND LIFE

Edifice of life stands on the base of love
Life without love an empty vessel, useless to rob
No love no life, no life no love intermingled inseparable
Love moves life to forward and downward inevitable.
Life is the storehouse of love to preserve
Natural imperishable wealth to serve
Mankind can rethink and reset to observe
What is essential the potion of life.
Life becomes chaotic without the presence of love
Rude and cruel enough to betray the near and dear
Powerless, meaningless to cheer
Let not life to ruin the gift of god, time to endear.
Life without you is like a fish out of water
Leaving you behind how I can stay better
Love and life two sides of the same coin
Let's come forward and take needful action to join.

76. DOING AT LEAST SOMETHING

Humans are workers by passion by nature,

Doers of verities of deeds and misdeeds to capture

Born with works of diverse shades of life to culture

To fill the blank paper of life one after the other in rapture

Doing at least something naturally does nurture.

Everyday inspires us to labour for livelihood

Works only makes us specified in staging manhood

Makes life live and grow providing sumptuous food

Lack of works leaves one rude and crude to brood

Doing at least something can soothe angry mood.

Yes, doing at least something matters a lot to book a slot

For a classic novel of life creates a marvelous plot

Unless and until sweating and bleeding run out of cut

Underestimate not your lot.

77. A RAY OF LIGHT

A ray of light gives a ray of hope to proceed

In the dark of loneliness requires what we need

Fortitude and faith upon oneself a potion in deed

Light in loneliness nurtures our mind to take heed.

Demon of dark can never tempt our self confidence

Mind gets stronger, sharper in patience and persistence

No deadly fright of night threatens being nimble in silence

Light lightens the tense of brain lighting the lamp of acceptance.

Bravery lies in making life a tourch

Things around us tremble in hotchpotch

And leave the way we walk along ahead as such

The finale of race wins with much applause.

78. BENEFITS OF JOINT FAMILY

Family of love bonding
Makes everything possible
A pillar of support binding
Things get easier and suitable.
No problems remain unsolved
No stones left unturned
Knot of hope ties together
Courage piles to gather.
Snow of difficulty melts away
Nobody or nothing can go astray
Ripples of happiness sway
Amidst all huddles on the way.
Place of sharing, caring and daring
Each other extends hands helping
Love, loyalty, faith, integrity abiding
One another dreaming of doing better and inspiring.

79. TRUTH VS LIES

Truth is light lies darkness
Dark can never cover truth
Without lies never lies truth
Both take the same mouth.
Both are close to each other
Having two ways communication
Separate destination varied action.
Truth ephemeral lies transient
Truth divine lies omnipresent
At the very outset truth fails
Nobody wants to know details
Truth slowly, gently triumphs at last
Lies gergeously spreads very fast.
Millions of fans in company of lies
Truth fights for the best with few guys
To dominate, powerful is hidden lies
Lies is like a mask to hide the scars.
Truth is bitter friend lies sweet enemy
Both of them have their own ceremony.
Truth is white, lies black
Truth key to open the door of lies
Lies sometimes help to rescue the truth from crisis
Truths are not truth that kills a life
Lies are not lies that save a life. They are two branches from the same tree.

80. ORIGINALITY

Open access to the world
Sparkling like diamond forever
Even in the dark twinkles more
Moon among the stars in azure.
As pure as water, the thirsty knows better
As transparent as mirror, nothing to flatter
The malafide sway in helter skelter
When the purity and integrity to glitter.
Nothing can be replaced however accurate
There's nothing credit in being perfect
Both are the imitation to say with no suspect
No respect when the root loses ensuing prospect.
Originality never mingles with duplication
That's the speciality, no need of confirmation
Before the eyes of beholders fail to prove justification
Everything in original rises from destruction.

81. MUSIC TO MY EARS

Like an electric power recharges my slackness
A source of serene happiness
Heart starts humming to the music
Mesmerizes me, o what a magic.
Life enlivens in the mellifluous tune
Rhythm of sound ripples inside
Drives away my anger and anxiety
I soar in the chariot of divinity.
My whole body warms up to dance
As if intoxicated to forget trance
Roaming in europhia of utopia
It works for me more than panacea.
Some music to my ears when I hear
Lasts long for years with no fear to cheer
Imprints in the slate of my heart dear
Wherever I am he is very near to bear.
Restoring in the store of my love enriches me
Enlightens, energizes and reshapes my destiny
Germs of my devilish attitude loses their existence
It is my life that teaches me to live in presence.

82. FOLIAGE OF LIFE

Like a massive tree life grows to the fullest
Amidst sun, rain, coolness and the worst and the best
Still longs for spreading hands helping and exploiting
Sometimes benevolent, sometimes arrogant in dreaming.
Life has myriads of crevices to hail fresh air of humanity
Limpid water of sanctity, tender and hotness of sun mighty
Gradually flourishing towards maturity helping to enrich
Each one of the hole of weakness to unleash out of reach.
Foliage of life preserves the outsourcing services for mankind
Every point and part needs something necessary behind
No matters whether be unkind or kind
Otherwise some of them inevitably are to rescind.
A life may pervades its branches of ephemeral solidarity
Hanging from the vacuum of nothingness in entity
Forbearance and the power of stamina in calamity
Brings plenty of gratitude and fortitude in tranquility.

83. WEDDING

Wedding Weds Two Souls
Part Becomes Whole
Welding worries and nostalgia
Often works more than panacea.
Ending the end of depression
Passing of age closes tension
Union of views and opinions
Intermingles in juxtaposition.
Over years of awaited desires
Flaming in the oven of flairs
Blazes with fun and social fairs
A promise, each other to care
A bond of love and affection
Where there's no pretension
Flicker of hope bonds together
Both of them free in al weather.
Two poles well in errection
Able to keep on institution
For forthcoming generation
A belief never faces extinction.

84. STORM IN LIFE

Storm in life is sure
Somehow it comes to cure
To make life pure
If one can endure.
It takes any form as it wishes
Trembles heart still blesses
Things are broken into pieces
Washes away some when gushes
Destroys the old to construct the new
Prepare a stage in due
Well decorated in diverse hue
Life sparkles like a drop dew
Hide not yourself from the storms
Boldly face it to accept the norms
Slowly flee away the adversity germs
Everything comes one by one in turn.

85. SPECIAL FRIENDS

Friends or foes both are special respectively
Friends are friends who can forget at a time positively
Foes are the bitter friends who always remember
Friends are close to friends in time of crisis, danger or even fest or luxury
In real sense are they source of strength in misery.
Foes are far away from the madding crowd to be unknown and unseen
Hidden treasure of earning warning and learning being enough keen
Sweet enemies strive to make injury so that one can opt the second option
Giving always a second chance to make the direction right, the evils to bury
How can I say they are not special who make my destiny
Ringing the bell of consciousness and without mutiny
Foes are not filtered to forget each step of growth and development
They are the real guide to show the path to travel
Blessings in disguise to marvel.

86. LOVE NEVER STOPS LOVING

Love hates, love loves, love ruins
Hate and love or love and hate, wins
Powerful flames twin twines
Like water and milk, like kith and kin
Inseparable, visibly invisible rapport thin.
Once indulged in bond never stops loving
No great wall of cement prevents nothing
Till last breath keeps on striving
Love for love rides on the highways of dreams.
Love blindly loves eloping far away from madding crowd
Love knows how to bear with situation feeling proud
From the eyes of the mob it can shroud
For the moment of euphoria love forgets the world.

87. BAD TIMES NEVER LAST LONG

88. CLOUDS

Cosmic carrier of rains
Fetches nector of pain
Piles of emotions to pen
Thousand hearts to train.
Messenger of hope
Seeding solace grain
Cuts the knots of rope
Unleashing grassy land.
Life enlivens in thy advent
Peacocks start twirling
In the whistling of gusty wind
Deep forest plays the violin.
Nature's charismatic drone
Wets in the shower of love
Often gets angry to ruin anything
To plant something mesmerising.

89. THE PURSUIT OF LOVE

A weapon to vanquish all social evils

What person you are love only reveal

Every heart can be won without fail

The paths of affection if you hail.

A source of joy and happiness

Can bind one and all in oneness

Fragrance of love spreads in selflessness

Without expectations and demand for own achievement.

A staunch belief in all respect

Brings closeness among all

A foundation on which stands the edifice ideals

But to pass the exam takes various ordeals.

An understanding to read nature and behavior

It is love that makes us superiors

A silent speaker of dedication and sacrifice.

Heart without love an empty vessel to share

Mo money, no power can easily compare

Anyone in pursuit of love a reformer

Love a guarantee card to reshape the destiny.

90. FRIENDSHIP DAY

A belief to believe blindly
A man needs a friend kindly
To gather fortitude in loneliness
To go ahead with togetherness.
A bond unbroken, unchallenged
Remains intact till nailing the coffin
It does not speak rather does more
Without expectations, without any return.

91. I HATE YOU

Because you are mine
I am at cloud nine
Even a little bit of you
Like more than my life.
I hate you
Because I like your dislikes
See in you the best
Feel in you the warmth.
I am angry with you
As I love you so much
I am in you to search
In every corner a torch.
I argue with you
Since am mesmerised
In thy mellifluous voice
In your reactions I rejoice.
I hate you to love you
As I want you love me too.

92. LOVE AFTER HATE

Love that doesn't love is love that lives decades after decades

That hides in the soft petals of hatred

No rose plucked without caressing thorn

After gloomy night only comes resplendent morn.

Love at first sight in long run fails to delight

As allured by outside beauty, inner self silently fight

Intoxicates the so called lovers dreaming at day light

Ocean of sorrows roars in the cacophony of ebb and tide.

Love after hate trains himself to calm down

Exploring the contemporary realm of ups and downs

Mistakes committed earlier teach them how to overcome battle

Company of togetherness gets nourished to lifelong settle.

Love born out of revulsion gets itself filtered

As cheese and ghee from milk mustered

Hate makes one angry, throws, burns and batters to be loved

In the decadence of contrition makes up mind to march forward.

93. POWER OF LOVE

Love is everywhere
As free as air
As limpid as water
Caters mankind better.
Love is as deadly as thunder
Burns the living tree of family
Innumerable lives it can murder
Like a python swallows slowly.
Like gusty wind ruins nests of dreams
Like furious flood topples down bridges of relations
When like the sun brightens whole world
Can also darken the future without notification.
Constructor and destructor conspicuous
Place, person time enables to serve the purpose
Love a game of hide and seek
Sometimes wins, sometimes falls sick.

94. EXPECTATIONS

No life exists without expectations
Expectations resides where life is
No one can be spared to botherations
When increases plenty of tribulations.
Life grows in the soil of expectations
With genuinely required proportion
That keeps the cart of life in motion
Bouncing life in reverberation.
But less expectations less tensions
And more expectations more dissatisfaction
The difference decides one's perception
Whether be a choice or an option.
Much expectations much corruption
Life soars in hallucinations
One day fall in the pit of destruction
Deduction of life with full confirmation.

95. BEAUTY OF NATURE

Unparalleled and indescribable the nature's beauty
That sows the seeds of serenity
Universalising the message of love peace and generosity
Oh, see how everything looks magnificent in tranquility.
Rays of the sun resplendent and mesmerising
Beholders sitting beside the sea shore feeling inspiring
When the tenderness of mighty sun caressing the sea so exciting
Especially during coming out and homecoming.
The water of the sea too agog turning cold or hot at the sun's advent
The east gets ready to give birth to the sunrise in vent
So is the west immensely mirthful in hiding in its lap for rest
With the play of hide and seek the whole world comes to grow and move.
Nature's Beauty is nature's ornaments sparkling forever
Emerging and staying unfaded and unhurt
Nurtures the earthly lives with charismatic power and divine bliss
Pervading the entire world in the canopy of enlightenment.

96. DARKNESS

The dark a mark of dislikeness
Neither preferred not proffered
Neither in gratifications nor in tribulations
Man of erudition remains in tenebrosity
Deep dark deeply mollycoddles
Spreading lap of germination
Say not and never an absurdiry
That gives a new life in exuberance
Dark clouds tear own heart to shower downpour
Life delighted in light takes birth in gloom.

97. YOU ONLY FAIL IF YOU QUIT

An action a process of efforts and execution

Incessant exploitation of continuation

Only criteria employed for possible acquisition

Incompleteness persists on quitting application

Let fear of failure flee away far in you introspection.

Regularizations with patience make things easier

Heart ripples in pleasure

Winning over uncertainty and complications

Flow of failure faints and fades in the world of operations

Final round is yours to explore the limitations.

Focus on one begets millionaire

Its reverse makes a man nugatory

Adherence to one is better than multipliers

Unsteadiness in words, thoughts or actions quite unfair

That topples down the tower of expectations in air

Leave not what once set up till you conquer.

98. THE PATH WE CHOOSE

Choosing a path is not easy
One must be choosy being crazy
Paths ahead full of diversions
The right one is uncertain
But we are compelled to obtain
One that is unknown
But making journey till last
Matters a lot nobody can forecast
No path is easy as one wishes
We have to make easier as to accomplish
Patience and perseverance together
Stands for those who love duty
Whichever path is taken further
If furnished with integrity
Then no chances of futility
One definitely able to gather
All ease and comfort anywhere
If he loves the path forever.

99. BUILD TODAY TO BUILD TOMORROW

Today is reality feel it, enumerate
It is in front of you no to exaggerate
Today is certainty, love, divinity
Today foundation builds with maturity
Every means of possibilities
Leave not this opportunity.
You can hold it as you see it
You can hug it as you near it
Today is yours treasure
Have its seraphic pleasure.
Today what you invest
Tomorrow you will harvest
Build Today to build Tomorrow
Better days reshaped to grow.
Today is light, tomorrow darkness
Today a plant needs watering
Today's nurture saves future
Suffer today, tomorrow will rapture.

100. WORLD PARENTS DAY

Someone

Who can blindly be believed?

Who can never ever deceive?

Who can without any clues perceive

They are parents

The living God and goddess to be worshipped

Someone

Unconditionally love till last breath

Who are lifelong hurt in the demise of offsprings

Who can go any extent for the their betterment

They are parents incarnation of creation

Whose debt can't be repaid by any possession?

Someone

Who likes both likes and dislikes

Who never get tired of days and nights toils

Who only think of goodness

They are parents unquestionable their actions

Incomparable their strength and sacredness

Someone

Who live for their children?

Who breathe for their generations

Who stand for family

They are parents the angels of reformation

Who needs to be cared with compassion

Who needs to be treated with

Love and affection

May they, as long as the world exists, live long

May they enliven to fulfill last wishes they long.

My heartfelt and humble gratitude to all the world parents they

belong.

101. WE ARE MADE TO REMAKE

WE are not born automatically
Over years of dreams dreamt
Actions of over decades planned
With hopes and beliefs cherished.
We are the fruits of prayers offered
Destination of someone's journey
Promises of someone's harmony
Celebration of awaited ceremony.
We are made up of blood and flesh
Sharp mind, soft heart a unique place
Sensed with rationality and grace
Filled with feelings and emotions
Enriched with great motion and potion.
Blessed with fire, water and air
All weather proof life to care
Much given to share
What needed is to dare.
We are the commitment already made
In sun umbrella to shade
Ointment to someone's wounds
Solutions to the problems found.
Ultimately we are made to remake something useful
For us, for others let it be unforgettable.
Don't complain what you are

We can rebuild by far.

102. NEVER LOSE THE KID IN YOU

Childishness the glory of humans
Moments of divinity pure domain
A period of absolute freedom
Nobody can conquer this kingdom.
More creative one in childhood
Concentrating mind the best mood
Simplicity and innocence his food
Enriches the wholeness of manhood.
A stage of fearlessness always sparkle
Beyond one's imagination it does miracle
No anger, envy or malafide intention can reach it
Never run after selfishness that can severely hurt.
Be a child to give farewell to discrimination
Speaking the language of love and affection
To lure the mind of myriads in gratification
Innocence a blessing, a wonder of creation.
Be a child to explore the world of dreams
The moment you have you can live life mirthful
Adversity in any kind or any form disappears like water bubble
No melancholy confronts, lose not your rubble
Feeble and ephemeral are all troubles.

103. LOVE WITH NO EXPECTATIONS

Love with expectation
Failure will break you, emotions smear
Absence will force eyes to shed tears
Aching pain you can't bear
So love without expectations
Let life live in full gratification.

Love with expectations
Captivates in the trap of illusion
Pushes beyond horizon
Drags away from the track of ambition
So love with no explanation
Let the world free from manipulation.

Love with expectations
Assures promises of fulfillment
Ensures betrayal, punishment
Invites to the grand finale
But defeats in the competition
So love with no expectations
Be self guide to overcome situations.

Love with no expectations
Life is full of diverse options
To pick up better destination
Love with no expectations
Love with no expectations.

104. WOMEN'S DAY, 2022

A day in a year to renew
What forgotten in a few
A day to remember again
Whether native or foreign.
See a woman in woman
Woman in a daughter twirls
Woman in a sister whirls
Woman in a man shrinks.
Feel the necessity of womanhood
It will complete your manhood
Can bloom flowers of childhood
Strengthen foundation of boy/girlhood.
Long for her long benign presence
Woman in a mother a deity human's essence
Goddess in a woman divine. worship
Woman in a goddess filled with sacredness.
Let woman be a woman, a better companion
Let's stand for her and stay behind a woman,
It is we who can make her champion
The future will ever see anything empyrean.

105. MAHASHIVRATRI

Mahadev, the lord of lords, unique style and get up always embellish
Among all a different God to flourish
Holder of Dambaru and Trishul to punish
Around his neck rests a snake to sting the naughty
Surrounded by hills and snowfall replete with serenity
Heads the mother Ganges to flood earth with nectar
In the time of calamities emerges as a saviour
Vigorously vested all power of construction and destruction
Resting in deep meditation wishes the welfare of the creation
Amalgam of twin flames of man and woman
Tri-eyed tridev image of sacrifices and devotion
Rescue the whole world from the devastation
Immensely kind and generous to His devotees
Happy Mahashivratri to one and all in merriment
Let it lit in the heart the lamp of enlightenment.

106. O DECEMBER

O, December,
Last but not the least to remember
Leaving some footprints to be followed forever
Some bitter, some sweet still near and dear to me
Miss you a lot but sanguine of meeting after a year.

107. POETS AND SCIENTISTS

All poets are scientists

Not all scientists are poets

All poets are inventors

Not all inventors are poets.

Unlike the scientists in the four walled laboratory

Poets make the whole world their factory

For manufacturing the products of words and imagery

Open the gate of mystery.

Unlike Scientists with proof and cerebration

Poets dwell in the world of fancy and imagination

Men of cogitation, contemplation, and concentration

Can reshape the future of the characters in itertextualization.

Peculiar are poets who can reach where others cannot

See what we can never imagine

Express what nobody can evince

Make the mountain move, the stone melt and what not

The emperor without any empire, the king without throne and crown

Rules over the world teaching what be out and what in

Carrying the message of divinity and immortality

For sustaining love, peace, harmony and humanity.

108. BEGINNING

Everything has a beginning

Each beginning a source of immense pleasure inspiring

Every day comes with a new beginning to aspire

Be the beginning of someone to respire.

Beloved and exciting a moment of remembrance.

Perpetually makes a home inside the core of heart

Blank page of life painted with colours if memories

Impels to set eyes on cherished goal.

Sows the seeds of perfection

Amidst the turmoils of Time's administration

Driving towards the end of a new beginning

Every ending has a beginning but no ending of a beginning.

109. CHARACTER

Character makes your destiny
More powerful than money
More sweeter than honey
Lessens the pain of journey.
Character triumphs everywhere
If free and fair
To defeat nobody is there
Care to make you rare.
Character is everything
Useless all possession and trifling
Paralysed if you are lacking
Save it from falling, sliding and rolling.
Character defends you, mends you right
No thunderbolt, no gusty shower bends you
No flood takes you away, no drought dries you tight
It can protect every mighty power or blow and fight.
Character makes your life joyful, peaceful
Happy and prosperous to live mirthful
Makes your life beautiful, resourceful
With what the future seeks forever needful.

110. WORLD PEACE DAY

You can have peace if you do and forget

You are happy if you cannot expect

You are honoured if you can respect

You are right if you learn from mistake

You are wrong if you think you are perfect

You cannot smile unless you cry

Earth cannot soak water unless it is dry

You are the only one you can give you peace

Doing one's duty is real source of divine bliss

Be what you are if you long for peace

Train yourself to calm down to make everything possible

Let things happen on its own way which is inevitable

Be simple to obtain the treasure of peace.